Science Discoveries

THOMAS

EDISON

and Electricity

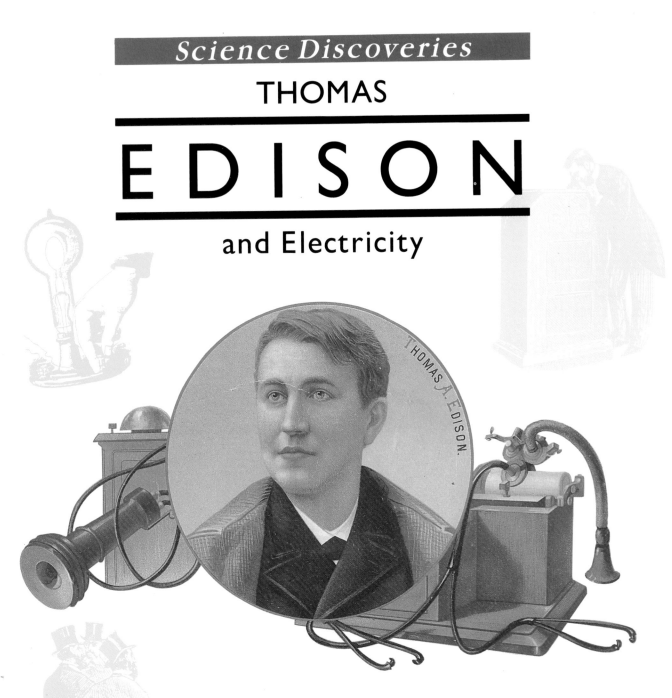

Steve Parker

Chelsea House Publishers
New York • Philadelphia

First published in Great Britain in 1992 by
Belitha Press Limited, 31 Newington Green, London N16 9PU.

First published in the USA by HarperCollins 1992.
This edition © Chelsea House Publishers 1995.

1 3 5 7 9 8 6 4 2

Library of Congress Cataloging-in-Publication Data
Parker, Steve
    Thomas Edison and electricity/Steve Parker.
        p.   cm.—(Science discoveries)
    Originally published: New York: HarperCollins, 1992.
    Includes bibliographical references and index.
    ISBN 0-7910-3012-1
    1. Edison, Thomas A. (Thomas Alva), 1847-1931—Juvenile
literature.   2. Inventors—United States—Biography—Juvenile
literature.   3. Electric engineering—United States—History—
Juvenile literature.   [1. Edison, Thomas A. (Thomas Alva),
1847-1931.   2. Inventors.]   I. Title.   II. Series: Science
discoveries (1994)
[TK140.E3P37   1995]
621.3'.092—dc20   94-20658
[B]   CIP
                                                            AC

Acknowledgments

Photographic credits:
Bridgeman Art Library, 17
Cincinnati Historical Society/Robert Harding
    Picture Library, 4
Mary Evans Picture Library, title page, 13 top,
    19 left, 23 top, 24 top
Illustrated London News Picture Library,
    25 bottom
The Image Bank, 9 top right Jake Rajs, 27 Marvin
    E. Newman
The Library of Congress, 6 right

Mansell Collection, 16 bottom, 23 bottom,
    24 middle
National Portrait Gallery, London, 8
Nelson Gallery, Atkins Museum, Kansas
    City/Robert Harding Picture Library, 7
Peter Newark's American Pictures, 6 left, 9
    bottom right, 10, 12, 14 top, 16 top, 20, 22
    bottom left, 24 bottom
Ann Ronan Picture Library, 21 top
Science Photo Library/J.L. Charmet, 13 bottom
U.S. Department of the Interior, National Park
    Service, Edison National Historic Site, 5 top,
    11 top, 22 top
U.S. Department of the Interior, National Park
    Service, Edison National Historic Site/Robert
    Harding Picture Library, 5 bottom, 9 left,
    11 bottom, 15 top, 21 bottom, 22 bottom
    right, 25 top, 26

Cover montage images supplied by Mary Evans
Picture Library and Ann Ronan Picture
Library

Illustrations:
Rodney Shackell, 19
Tony Smith, 14–15, 18

Printed in China for Imago

Contents

Introduction

Imagine what life would be like without electric lights or record players, telephones or movies. Imagine no power stations, or the pylons, cables, and wires that bring electricity to our homes, factories, offices, and schools.

Thomas Edison, the "greatest inventor of his age," was central to all these developments. In the years between 1870 and 1920, Edison and his coworkers came up with hundreds of useful devices and machines, mostly run by electricity. They ranged from a giant kiln (oven) for making cement to one of the most familiar items in any home—the electric light bulb.

Edison rarely came up with a completely new invention. His talents lay in taking the ideas and inventions of others and improving them. His engineering and fault-finding skills made machinery more efficient and reliable. He showed how devices and processes could be used successfully on a large scale to solve problems, to speed up communications and manufacturing, and generally to improve life.

An early photograph of Cincinnati, Ohio, taken in 1848, the year after Edison's birth. It shows a world of steam engines and gas lamps, very different from the world of electric light bulbs and automobiles that Edison would leave behind in 1931.

4

Chapter One
The Early Years

The house where Thomas Alva Edison was born in Milan, Ohio.

On February 11, 1847, in Milan, Ohio, Thomas Alva Edison was born. His family lived in a small house near the Lake Erie shore. Thomas' father, Samuel, was in the timber business. He and his wife, Nancy, had seven children altogether, but three died at a young age. When Thomas was a baby, his surviving brother and sisters were already teenagers.

A problem pupil

In 1854, at the age of seven, Thomas and his family moved to Port Huron, on the southern tip of Lake Huron. His father's business had failed, and the family had little money. About this time Thomas caught scarlet fever, which left him very hard of hearing. The next year he had the only formal schooling of his life. But his great curiosity, poor hearing, and tendency to play tricks soon got him into trouble. After only three months the schoolmaster said he was "retarded," and Nancy Edison took her son away from the school. No one suspected that Edison would be a multimillionaire within 22 years.

At the age of 12 Thomas declared himself to be grown up and independent, so he took a job selling food and newspapers on the railroad.

A deserved reward

Edison remembered his days on the railroad as the happiest time of his life. His poor hearing usually meant he had trouble hearing others' speech. But he could hear passengers' shouting above the noise of the train. And he could hear the high-pitched click of the telegraph machine as it printed out messages in the dots and dashes of Morse code.

He once rescued the son of a telegraph agent from an oncoming train. As a reward, he was taught how to work the telegraph machine. It was the beginning of his career as a telegrapher and his interest in electrical machines.

The home chemistry set

His mother took over Thomas' education. He read books on philosophy and science, including one of the most famous science books of all time, Isaac Newton's *Principia Mathematica*. This gave him great respect for scientific theories, but began his dislike of mathematics. His imagination was caught mainly by chemistry and physics experiments. He set up a home laboratory in the household basement. He asked local shopkeepers for free jars and chemicals, and he copied the experiments he read about in science books.

In 1859 the Grand Trunk Railroad opened a line from Port Huron to Detroit. New railroads and telegraph lines were snaking across the land. Thomas got a job as a newsboy, selling newspapers on the trains. He soon enlarged his first business by selling candy and seasonal vegetables as well. He employed other boys at stations along the line, and he made enough money to buy more science books. The boy scientist even used a spare car on the train as a laboratory and a printing press for the passengers' newspaper, *The Grand Trunk Herald*, which he wrote himself.

The coming of the telegraph

Sending messages over long distances was difficult in a huge country like the United States. When Edison was a boy the pony express operated for a short while. Teams of riders and horses covered the 2,000 miles, from Missouri to California, in ten days. But messages sent as electrical signals along telegraph wires went at the speed of light, and in 1861 the pony express went out of business.

Tramp telegrapher

The Civil War began in 1861. A year later the telegraph operator in Port Huron went off to fight, and Edison took his job. Between sending and receiving messages, he continued his experiments in the basement of the office. At age 17 he took a telegraph job in Canada.

This was the beginning of a six-year career as a wandering "tramp telegrapher." These men were fast, skilled telegraph operators who worked wherever the wages were highest. Edison roamed the United States and Canada. He liked to work night shifts, so he could continue his scientific reading and experiments during the day. Sometimes his experiments got him into trouble because he made new machines from his employer's equipment. Several times he was fired.

Thomas would have worked on trains much like the one below. This picture was painted in 1860, when trains and wagon trails provided the main form of transportation in the U.S.

The importance of patents

A patent is a description of an invention. It is registered with the government to show who thought of it first. For a set period of time afterward, only the inventor can make, use, or sell the invention. The inventor can grant permission to others to do so, for a fee, or can sell the patent outright to others. A patent is important if an invention becomes successful, because the person who owns the patent makes the money.

New uses for electricity

In 1868 Edison took a job with Western Union telegraph in Boston. He won respect by taking down a message sent by the "fastest telegrapher in New York." But he was criticized because his writing was too small. In anger he filled each sheet of paper with a few huge words—and he was moved to another job.

At the age of 21, Edison read *Experimental Researches in Electricity* by Michael Faraday. Like him, Faraday was a self-taught scientist and experimenter with electricity. Edison was greatly encouraged. He began to write his ideas in notebooks, take more care with his methods, and record the results of his experiments. He also visited workshops in Boston where people were looking for new uses for electricity. Although various batteries and dynamos could make electricity, the telegraph was its only widespread use.

In 1868 Edison applied for his first patent, and it was granted the next year. It was for an automatic electrical vote counter, intended for U.S. Congress. But it was unsuccessful because officials were reluctant to use it. Edison never forgot this lesson: Never bother with inventions that people will not want!

Michael Faraday

Sometimes called the "father of electricity," Faraday worked during the first half of the nineteenth century. He experimented with chemicals such as chlorine, and he originated the concept of "lines of force" from a magnet. He was important in the development of the electric motor, generator, and transformer.

Chapter Two
The Budding Inventor

Edison realized that he wanted to work with electricity and machines. He wanted to invent and improve them. He left Western Union for the workshops of Charles Williams, a telegraph-instrument maker. Here he invented his first successful machine, a stock ticker.

In the financial world, people buy stock or shares in a company. This is like lending the company some money. If the company makes a profit, the people who own its stock share in that profit. Millions of dollars change hands. It is vital for such people to know which companies are doing well, and which shares are going up or down in price. Today this information is updated every second using computers, along telephone lines. In Edison's time messengers ran from one office to another.

Edison's stock ticker was an adaptation of the telegraph. It sent the latest stock prices electrically along wires to printers in other offices. (Like the telegraph, it made a clicking or ticking sound as it worked.) Like much of Edison's work, it was an improvement on an old system, not a new idea.

The ticker-tape parade

When parades pass through the financial district of New York City, marchers are showered with pieces of paper. When this tradition started, people threw the narrow ribbons of paper from their stock tickers. Hence the name—"ticker-tape parade."

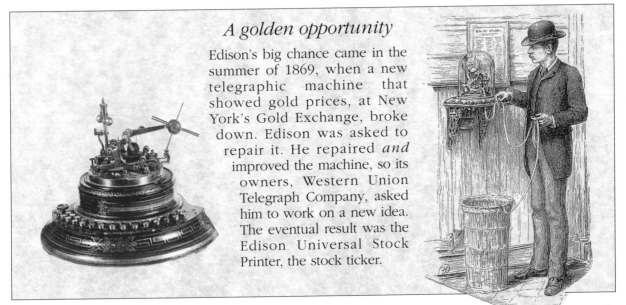

A golden opportunity

Edison's big chance came in the summer of 1869, when a new telegraphic machine that showed gold prices, at New York's Gold Exchange, broke down. Edison was asked to repair it. He repaired *and* improved the machine, so its owners, Western Union Telegraph Company, asked him to work on a new idea. The eventual result was the Edison Universal Stock Printer, the stock ticker.

An engraving of the Gold Room in New York City, where gold was bought and sold. Edison's stock ticker was used to communicate new prices for gold to other offices around New York.

Early business ventures

Leaving Boston, Edison moved to New York and took a job in a gold recorder's office in the city's financial district. He worked on new systems for sending gold prices and stock prices between offices. The dealers who could get the latest prices fastest could make more money, by selling or buying ahead of their competitors.

But Edison was soon on the move again. He started a business with Franklin Pope: Pope, Edison and Company, Electrical Engineers. They advertised that they could "devise electrical instruments and solve problems to order."

In one of his first big business deals, Edison earned $5,000 for selling the patent to his improved stock ticker and gold printer to Western Union. The same organization paid him the then-enormous sum of $40,000 for the patent to an even better stock printer in 1870. One of the improvements was that a faulty or jammed printer could be restarted by sending special "unjamming" electrical signals along the wire.

With this great amount of money, Edison decided to set up a factory for making his inventions.

Edison's factory on Ward Street, Newark, New Jersey.

Chapter Three

Edison the Businessman

Mary Stilwell in the year of her marriage, age 16.

By 1871 Edison opened his own workshop and factory on Ward Street in Newark, New Jersey, to manufacture stock tickers and other equipment, and to develop new electrical devices. He employed two shifts of workers and soon opened other workshops. He was 24.

Edison worked incredibly hard. He took charge of all the projects and hardly ever slept. He expected his workers to do the same! Many did because Edison set a good example. He showed great enthusiasm and always had plenty of ideas for new devices.

He was not so successful in managing his business matters. He opened a bank account to deposit the $40,000, but he kept track of his finances with two nails in the wall—where he stuck all his bills and payments.

The Edison family

On Christmas Day, 1871, Edison married Mary Stilwell, a 16-year-old worker at his factory. Their first child, Marion, was born the next year. She was nicknamed Dot, from the dots and dashes of Morse code. In 1876 their son Thomas was born—and nicknamed Dash! Another son, William, followed in 1878.

A confusion over patents

Edison spent time and money on projects that were not successful at first. He ran into debt. At last in 1874 he perfected a system of sending several messages at the same time and in both directions by telegraph between New York, Boston, and Philadelphia.

But there was a legal argument about who owned the patents. In an attempt to pay his debts, Edison had been working for both Western Union and Atlantic & Pacific. Both companies thought Edison was creating the new system exclusively for them. Edison became embroiled in a lengthy court battle, after which he resolved to keep patents more under his own control.

Faster communications

For another payment of $40,000, Edison and his team worked for the Automatic Telegraph Company. For two years he worked on machines that eventually could transmit accurate messages at 200 words per minute—six times faster than the quickest telegraph operator. He went to England to sell the system to the post office there. While there he tried to send messages across the Atlantic Ocean between the United States and Britain, but the tests that he did failed.

The telephone

In 1876 one of Edison's fellow inventors took out patents on a new device. Instead of sending dots and dashes or similar signals along a wire, it converted the sounds of the human voice into electrical signals and transmitted these. It was the first telephone, and its inventor was Alexander Graham Bell.

Rival companies realized how important the invention was. Edison was hired by Western Union to make a better version. He soon designed a system that used tiny granules of carbon in a small container or "button." As the granules were pressed together by the sound waves of a voice, the amount of electricity passing through them varied. The carbon-button telephone transmitter was successfully tested between New York and Philadelphia, and the patent was applied for in 1877. There was a 15-year delay before the patent was granted, and by then Bell's system was well established.

Edison's designs for the carbon-button telephone transmitter (left) and receiver (right). The transmitter changes the voice into electric signals and the receiver converts these back to a recognizable voice.

part of carbon transmitter

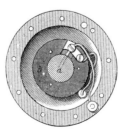

the inside of a receiver

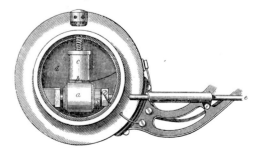

Alexander Graham Bell speaking into the mouthpiece of his version of the telephone, which he patented in 1876.

Bell's telephone

Instead of carbon granules, Bell's telephone used the principle of electromagnetism. The sound waves hit a flat sheet, or diaphragm, of very thin metal and made it vibrate. As the diaphragm moved, the magnetic field of a nearby magnet was altered. In turn, the changing magnetic field created electrical signals in a coil of wire wrapped around the magnet. The electrical signals passed along the wire to the earpiece of the telephone at the other end, the prototype of which is shown here, where the whole process was reversed to make sound waves again.

Chapter Four
The Empire at Menlo Park

In 1876 Edison moved to Menlo Park, a small town about 24 miles from New York City. He bought a house and built a large laboratory and workshop, including a machine shop for making parts, a carpenter's shop, and later a library. He gathered about 20 of his best workers around him. They were busy day and night, ate only when they were hungry, and slept only when they needed to. They were carried along by the thrill of invention. Edison often slept at his desk.

Menlo Park was an "invention factory." Edison and his workers did not make instruments in large numbers, as on Ward Street. At this time Edison preferred to leave manufacturing to those he called "robber barons," men who bought patents from inventors for small sums and made millions for themselves.

The team designed new machines and devices to solve specific problems. Ideas came to Edison all the time. He made endless notes and sketches and worked on several projects at once—sometimes as many as 40. In his working life he filled 3,400 notebooks.

Working hard

Edison was known as a hard taskmaster. He worked extremely hard and expected his employees to do the same. He himself summarized their working conditions by saying, "We don't pay anything and we work all the time." Once when a project was not working properly, he told his staff, "I've locked the door, and you'll have to stay here until this job is completed." He could get away with this because he himself worked hardest of all. In 1888 he spent a nonstop 72-hour stint working to improve the phonograph.

Toward the phonograph

In 1877, when Edison was working on his telephone system, he tried an experiment. The diaphragm of the telephone was a flat plate that vibrated when sound waves hit it. He tried to record its vibrations by linking it to a stylus, which pressed into paper. He rigged up a machine and recorded the word "halloo" as dents in the paper. When the marked paper was pulled back through, it moved the stylus, which vibrated the diaphragm, which produced sound waves in the air. As Edison said, with "strong imagination" the original word was heard again.

Edison was spurred on by reports that others were working on the same type of machine. He designed a machine with a recording cylinder covered not with paper but with metal foil. This was built by his colleague John Kruesi in December 1877. It worked. One of Edison's first recordings on his new invention, the phonograph, was "Mary Had a Little Lamb."

In 1878 Edison took his phonograph to the National Academy of Sciences.

Menlo Park was set up by Edison in 1876 and became one of the first invention factories, where inventors worked in teams to come up with new ideas and improvements. Later Edison lit the grounds of Menlo Park with electric bulbs (see page 19).

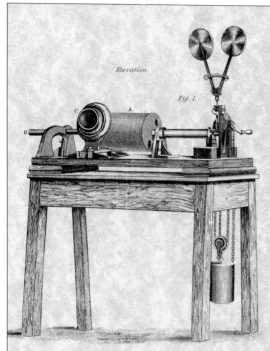

Elevation

Fig. 1.

The phonograph

The principle of the phonograph remained the same for many years, but the machinery soon changed. Wax cylinders replaced the foil ones, and copies of the recording were made by molding. But they soon wore out.

In 1887 a rival engineer, Emile Berliner, developed a recording made on a flat disc. The sound pattern was in a tiny wavy groove. The playback diaphragm became a big horn-shaped loudspeaker. The system was still mechanical—it did not use electricity to amplify the vibrations or the sound signals. But the disc was more convenient, easier to copy, and gave better sound quality than Edison's version.

Gradually discs took over from cylinders, and much later came the LP (long-playing) record, made out of vinyl plastic. In 1912 Edison himself gave up on cylinders and used discs for his phonographs.

The phonograph, known then as the talking machine, created a big stir. Edison enjoyed showing people what it could do and proving that it was not a hoax. He became known as the "Wizard of Menlo Park."

Chapter Five
Let There Be Light

A painting from the middle of the nineteenth century shows a family supper lit by an oil lamp.

In the 1870s some houses had gas lights. Other people used candles or oil lamps—or they went to bed at dusk. The only electric lights were arc lights, whose glow came from an arc or "spark" of electricity jumping continuously between pieces of carbon. Some important buildings had arc lights. But they shone for only a few hours before they had to be replaced. Also, they gave a very concentrated glare that was too bright to look at.

The glow bulb

Edison visited the arc-light exhibition of William Wallace and took up the invention of a "safe, mild, and inexpensive" electric lamp as his next target. Moreover, he intended to set up a system of electricity generators and wires and cables, like the gas-pipe network, to bring electricity to everyone. He obtained money from businessmen and set up the Edison Electric Light Company.

In 1878 he applied for his first patent in the search for a glass "glow bulb." It described a filament made of platinum, a hard metal that could withstand very high temperatures. There was also an electrical governor to prevent the platinum from overheating.

Electricity was passed through the filament to make it glow white-hot—giving off light. But a white-hot filament burns itself out quickly in open air. Oxygen combines with the filament and turns it to ash—just as it would with a piece of burning coal. Edison encased the filament in a glass bulb and created a vacuum by pumping out the air, so the filament would last much longer.

One percent inspiration

Edison prided himself on being a "commercial inventor." He enjoyed scientific research, but not for its own sake. He wanted to devise things that would make people's lives easier—and that would make money. He realized that this meant long hours of patient observation and experiments, taking notes and trying alternatives. He might be helped by the occasional flash of insight. His famous saying was that "genius is one percent inspiration, ninety-nine percent perspiration."

17

When Edison turned his attention to the potential of electric lighting, he boasted that it would take him only six weeks to invent an electric light bulb that would not have all the disadvantages of arc lights. In fact it took him almost a year. The picture shows Edison and his coworkers in the laboratory at Menlo Park working on the electric light bulb.

White-hot cotton

Edison and his team developed a new vacuum pump to make better vacuums in the glass bulbs. They also experimented with hundreds of materials for the filaments. They gave up on metal and made one from specially treated, carbonized cotton thread. Between October 21 and 22, 1879, the second of these new bulbs burned for 40 hours—a success! Edison at once applied for a patent. On New Year's Eve, 1879, the Menlo Park streets and houses were lit with 30 of the new bulbs.

In London the chemist and inventor Joseph Swan had been working along the same lines as Edison for 20 years. He also developed a carbon filament and vacuum bulb. Swan formed the Swan United Electric Light Company Limited. More battles over patents loomed, but in 1883 the Edison and Swan companies joined, and the patent battle was solved.

In the meantime, Edison quickly applied for dozens of patents: for electric lights, for the equipment used to make them, and for the distribution of electricity. The light bulbs themselves were continually improved. Bamboo fibers took the place of cotton, and years later cellulose was used.

The different designs for the light bulbs: one invented by Edison, one by Swan.

Making nothingness

In one type of vacuum pump, a piston sucks air out of the bulb through an open valve, while the valve to the air outside is closed. Then the piston moves back again, pushing the air out of the pump, while the valve to the bulb is shut. After many pumps, nearly all the air is removed from the bulb.

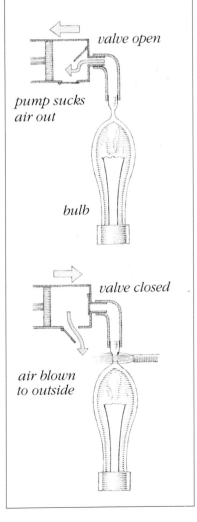

valve open

pump sucks air out

bulb

valve closed

air blown to outside

Edison light bulb

Swan light bulb

The dynamo room in Edison's electric-light station, 1882.

The first district

The Pearl Street power station had Edison-designed generators driven by steam engines. The station supplied enough electricity to light 1,200 bulbs, and its cables served an area of about one square mile, known as the First District. On opening day it had 52 customers. The lamps began to glow at 3 P.M. on September 4, 1882. It was a historic moment, and business boomed from the first day.

The power of light

If electric lights were to light every home, Edison knew there had to be a system for making and distributing electricity. His team was soon working on this.

Businesspeople rapidly realized that if they could light their offices and factories brightly, they could get far more work done, especially in the dark winter. Lighting systems were installed for newspaper offices and photographic companies as well as private houses. Early systems were troublesome and needed many repairs, but they were quickly improved. By the early 1880s there were five electric-light companies (including Edison's) trying to light up New York.

The first power station

Edison next concentrated on the source of electricity itself—the dynamo or generator. He improved existing designs, making them twice as efficient at turning the energy in their fuel into electrical energy. His team provided lighting for the first French Electrical Exposition in Paris. After this success Edison set up electric-light companies in France, England, Italy, Holland, and Belgium.

The year of 1882 was a milestone. The Edison company exhibited an artistic lighting display at the Crystal Palace in London. And more than 100,000 electric light bulbs were manufactured that year to satisfy the rocketing demand.

Edison and his advisers found places to manufacture dynamos, lamps, and cables. They also chose the site for the world's first real power station and the area to be served by it, in Manhattan, New York City. This was Pearl Street, where Edison's power station and electricity system were turned on in September 1882.

Despite great success, and more power stations, and more electric-light systems, Edison's money kept running out. Some was lost due to poor business methods, and the rest was spent on yet more experiments and inventions.

Edison's creative vision sensed that some things could be possible. For example, he imagined flying in machines like the one above and in contraptions more like helicopters. However, it was other inventors of that time who pursued these dreams.

Family tragedy

In 1884 Edison's wife Mary died of typhoid. On top of this tragedy, in the following year he began the first of more than 200 legal battles to try to stop others from copying his lighting equipment. This took nearly ten years and cost him $2,000,000. In the meantime he looked at the possibilities of making a flying machine (today we would call it a helicopter), but he was badly burned in an accident and gave up.

Edison with some of his electric bulbs that produced the "Edison effect" (see page 26).

Mina Edison and daughter Madeleine. She was 19 when she married Edison.

Chapter Six
A New Life

Two years after Mary's death, Edison married again. His second wife was Mina Miller, and they had three children, Madeleine, Charles, and Theodore. Edison decided it was time for change. He was now a famous businessman and he was less willing to spend long hours in the lab. He bought Glenmont, a house in West Orange, New Jersey, and built new laboratories, workshops, and factories that were ten times bigger than Menlo Park.

Edison and his teams worked on an improved phonograph with a floating stylus, an electric motor, and wax cylinders. The West Orange factory made dolls with tiny phonographs inside them, which played nursery rhymes.

Edison was now a world figure. He met heads of state and famous scientists in Europe, founded a recording company, and developed a dictaphone (a small machine for recording speech, to be typed later).

The Edisons' new home, Glenmont, in West Orange, New Jersey. Here Mina was able to make sure that Thomas spent more time with his family and not so much at work.

An advertisement for the Edison talking doll, an example of one of the uses the phonograph was put to in 1890.

WE ARE NOW PREPARED
TO SUPPLY THE

EDISON TALKING DOLL

EDISON'S TALKING DOLL.

TO THE TRADE ONLY.

For Wholesale Price and Terms, Address

EDISON PHONOGRAPH TOY MFG. CO.,

No. 138 FIFTH AVENUE, NEW YORK.

The photographer Eadweard Muybridge came to West Orange to demonstrate his "moving pictures." He and Edison discussed the possibility of linking recorded pictures to the recorded voice. In 1888 Edison took out patents on his kinetoscope, an early piece of movie equipment. A coworker, William Dickson, showed him a movie picture with sound—one of the earliest "talkies." But the equipment had problems, and the Edison team went on to other projects. Real talkies did not begin until 1927.

Eadweard Muybridge, an English photographer, was famous for his studies of animal motion.

The birth of motion pictures

Edison is sometimes said to have invented motion pictures, the movie camera, and the movie projector.

In fact, they were the work of several people, including members of his companies.

• Eadweard Muybridge first showed that the idea was feasible with his pictures of running horses.

• Edison's colleague William Dickson tried to record the pictures on wax cylinders.

• Then Dickson used the new flexible celluloid film, devised by George Eastman, for the kinetograph and kinetoscope.

• In 1893 Black Maria, the world's first movie studio, was set up at Glenmont. Kinetoscopes were installed in New York to show the resulting films.

• Edison did not think the kinetograph and kinetoscope would become hugely successful, so he did not protect them by patents in Europe.

• In the 1890s in France, Louis and Auguste Lumière further improved Edison's machines. Soon there were dozens of inventors working on improved versions of motion-picture cameras and projectors.

Edison's laboratory at West Orange. It shows the inside of the kinetographic theater with a phonograph and kinetograph being used at the same time to achieve a film with sound.

Toward the 20th century

Henry Ford in his first car, built in 1892.

In the last years of the nineteenth century Edison and his companies were busy, as always. The discovery of X rays in 1895 was soon followed by a better screen to detect and photograph them—designed by Edison. At the New York debut of Edison's fluoroscope, people could view their bones! He rushed through new versions of movie-film projectors and talking pictures. Henry Ford, a worker in one of Edison's companies, built his first and second automobiles. He would later found the Ford Motor Company.

Radio and electronics

Edison's storage battery was able to power a car. It was completed in 1902.

The twentieth century saw the first "wireless" radio messages sent across the Atlantic Ocean, by Guglielmo Marconi. Edison sent his congratulations, sold Marconi his patent on wireless telegraphy from 1885, and said: "That fellow's work put him in my class." The great era of radio and electronics was beginning. Edison lacked knowledge about the details of how electricity really worked, and he was too busy with his big industrial projects to get involved.

For many years, Edison worked on electrical cells (more commonly called batteries). He invented the alkaline storage battery, which could be recharged.

Marconi with the first apparatus he built for telegraphy without wires in 1896.

The Last Years

One of Edison's last projects was to find an alternative to the rubber available then only from British-owned rubber plantations. He wanted American rubber-using industries to be independent. After breeding many new types of plants, he came up with a type of giant goldenrod that produced latex rubber. But others were working on artificial rubber, and the goldenrod rubber never went into production.

Apart from his partial deafness, Edison had always enjoyed good health despite his hundreds of late-night sessions in the laboratory. In 1929 Henry Ford organized a celebration of fifty years of electric lights, with a new Museum of History that contained the rebuilt laboratory from Menlo Park. Edison attended the celebrations with President Herbert Hoover. He was 82. After this, his health began to fail.

Through 1930 and 1931 Edison fought illness. In his last public message he said: "I have lived a long time. . . . Have faith. Go forward." He died on October 18, 1931, after suffering from diabetes and a kidney problem called Bright's disease.

The First World War

When World War I began in Europe in 1914, Edison suggested that the armed forces should have a research laboratory to develop better weapons. He became chairman of the Navy Consulting Board, which had members from the best research organizations in America. He imagined a war where soldiers operated killing machines rather than fighting each other hand to hand. As busy as ever, he also developed torpedo-detecting devices and antisubmarine devices.

Above, Edison naps during one of his camping trips with President Harding and Harvey Firestone (one of the leading manufacturers of rubber tires) in 1921.

Edison in his later years.

The commercial side of Edison's style of practical science is shown in this amazing advertisement for light bulbs.

Chapter Seven

Edison in Perspective

Edison's inventions and improvements were only part of his great contribution to modern life, which ranged from electrical engineering and chemistry to transportation, entertainment, and the comforts of daily living.

Edison's life was a "rags to riches" story. He had little formal schooling in science or business. Yet through good sense, a busy and questioning mind, and sheer hard work, he gained fame and fortune. He was granted an amazing 1093 patents during his lifetime.

Research and development

The teams and working methods that Edison set up at Menlo Park were the first of their kind. Other organizations soon followed the idea of bringing together experts in different branches of science, to carry out experiments and work together in a step-by-step way on new projects. Today we call these activities "research and development." No major company can expect to succeed without them.

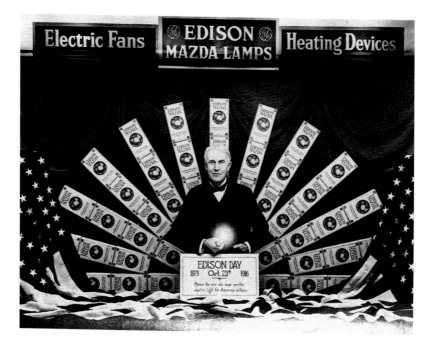

A scientist at heart

Edison's notebooks show that he understood many of the principles of science, despite his lack of training. He also followed the scientific method—having ideas, testing them, analyzing and explaining the results, and proposing further tests based on the results.

Edison was part old-time inventor, who loved working long hours in the laboratory, and part modern businessman, setting up teams of experts and reinvesting the profits from his companies in further research. When he was born, in the time of the candle and oil lamp, the world was in the "dark ages." By the time of his death, the modern age of machines and technology and electronics was well under way.

On October 21, 1931, America paid tribute to the "Wizard of Menlo Park" at his funeral. For one full minute the lights were turned off and electrical equipment was shut down all across the nation. Imagine New York City with no lights. The lights have never been off since and the magnificence of New York at night is one of Edison's legacies to us today.

The World in Edison's Time

	1847–1875	1876–1900
Science	**1847** Thomas Edison is born **1859** Charles Darwin publishes *On the Origin of Species* **1861** Physicist James Maxwell makes the first color photograph	**1882** First hydroelectric plant built, in Wisconsin **1883** The United States is divided into four time zones, as suggested by the railroad companies **1893** Rudolf Diesel works on the first internal combustion engine
Western Expansion and Exploration	**1853** First railway lines and telegraph cables laid in India **1859** First oil well drilled in Pennsylvania **1869** First ever transcontinental railroad completed in the United States	**1877** Queen Victoria proclaimed Empress of India **1888** Scandinavian explorer Fridtjof Nansen and his team complete the first land crossing of Greenland **1898** The U.S. annexes Hawaii
Politics	**1848** Karl Marx and Friedrich Engels write *Communist Manifesto* **1861** American Civil War begins **1865** President Abraham Lincoln assassinated at the theater	**1899** Boer War begins in southern Africa **1900** Boxer Rebellion in China
Arts	**1854** Henry David Thoreau writes *Walden* **1860s** French painter Claude Monet begins to produce his most famous works, known as impressionistic paintings **1873–75** French composer Georges Bizet writes his most famous opera, *Carmen*	**1879** A young Spanish girl and her father discover the now-famous prehistoric cave paintings at Altamira, Spain **1885** Mark Twain publishes *Huckleberry Finn* **1896** Chemist Alfred Nobel dies, and the five annual Nobel Prizes for physics, chemistry, medicine, literature, and peace are endowed through his will

1901-1925	1926-1950
1903 Wilbur and Orville Wright make the first heavier-than-air aircraft flight	**1928** Scottish microbiologist Alexander Fleming discovers a mold that makes a substance he calls penicillin—the first antibiotic drug
1905 Albert Einstein begins his work on the Theory of Relativity	**1931** Thomas Edison dies
1919 Ernest Rutherford splits the atom	**1948** An American team invents the transistor
1902 The first telegraph cable is laid under the Pacific	**1927** American aviator Charles Lindbergh makes the first nonstop transatlantic solo flight in *Spirit of St. Louis*
1911 Roald Amundsen is the first to reach the South Pole	
1914 Panama Canal opens	
1914–18 World War I	**1929** Wall Street crash precipitates world Depression
1916 The U.S. enacts its first child labor law	**1939–45** World War II
1917 The Russian Revolution begins	**1948** In the Middle East the new Jewish state named Israel is established
	1949 Apartheid program inaugurated in South Africa
1904 Anton Chekhov, Russian playwright, finishes *The Cherry Orchard*	**1927** Al Jolson stars in *The Jazz Singer*, the first movie released with a simultaneous sound track
1911 Composer Irving Berlin writes an early jazz song, "Alexander's Ragtime Band"	**1929** English author D. H. Lawrence writes *Lady Chatterley's Lover*
	1936 Russian composer Sergei Prokofiev completes his musical fairy tale *Peter and the Wolf*

Glossary

Bright's disease: An acute disease of the kidneys causing inflammation and eventual deterioration of these organs.

carbon: a natural substance that occurs in many forms, from diamonds to coal, charcoal, and soot. Solid carbon (which makes up a lot of the "lead" in a pencil) lets a certain amount of electricity pass through it. Carbon granules are small, black, sootlike specks.

cellulose: a natural substance made by plants. It is often long and stringy, and is contained in fibers such as cotton, jute, and flax. It was eventually used for the filament in the light bulb.

diabetes: a medical condition in which the body cannot use its natural sugars properly. Untreated, diabetes may cause drowsiness, unconsciousness, and even death.

diaphragm: a flat flexible sheet or plate, often made of very thin metal, which usually can move to and fro, or shake, or vibrate. The part of a loudspeaker that moves to and fro, making soundwaves, is one example of a diaphragm.

dynamo: a machine for making electricity. A type of generator.

engineering: the science of designing, making, putting together, and maintaining machines and structures, from a pair of scissors to a jumbo jet.

filament: a long, thin, threadlike part or structure, such as the thin piece of wire that glows in an electric light bulb, or a single strand of a substance such as nylon.

generator: a machine that makes electricity from some other form of energy, such as the heat given off by burning coal or oil, or the power of rushing water, or nuclear fuel, or the heat or light of the sun.

governor: in engineering, a device that controls or limits the movements of part of a machine. In a steam engine, the governor controls the turning speed of the flywheel so that it does not rotate too quickly or too slowly.

kinetograph: an early type of motion-picture camera, developed by Thomas Edison. It did not take photographs as clearly or as quickly as later movie cameras. It was named from the word "kinetic," which means "having to do with motion."

kinetoscope: an early piece of motion-picture equipment developed by Thomas Edison. It was a large box containing a long roll of movie film that went round and round, watched by one person through a hole or binocular-type eyepieces. See also kinetograph.

Morse code: a code of short electrical signals (dots) and long ones (dashes) that stand for letters and words. For example, the letter S is represented by dot-dot-dot. It was invented by Samuel Morse in about 1838, for use on the telegraph.

patent: a description of an invention, registered with a government agency to show who thought of it first, thus protecting the rights of the inventor.

piston: part of an engine that is forced back and forth inside a cylinder by some pressure such as combustion.

telegraph: a device for sending messages over long distances along electrical wires, usually in the form of a code such as on-off signals or the dots and dashes of Morse code.

transmit: to send or beam out. A television satellite transmits TV signals to the Earth from space, and a telegraph transmits electrical signals along a wire.

vacuum: nothingness—a place where there is nothing, not even air. Most of space is a vacuum. It is not generally possible to have a perfect vacuum, where there really is nothing at all. There are usually very small amounts of gases or other substances floating about.

valve: a device within a cylinder that permits a flow in one direction only or otherwise regulates the flow of whatever is in the cylinder.

Index

STEVE PARKER has written more than 40 books for children, including several volumes of the Eyewitness series. He has a bachelor of science degree in zoology and is a member of the Zoological Society of London.